SUCCESSFUL MANAGEMENT

A Practical Guide to Becoming A More Successful Manager

Herbert M. Levin

Copyright © 2019 by Herbert M Levin

All rights reserved. This book or any portion thereof may not be reproduced or used in any manner whatsoever without the express written permission of the publisher except for the use of brief quotations in a book review or scholarly journal.

First Printing: 2019

ISBN: 9781077655324

Herbert M Levin

822 Milam Ave.

Coral Gables, FL 33134

eMail: hmlconsultant2011@gmail.com

Dedication

I am in debt to the many talented, intelligent people with whom I have had the honor of working with and learning from over these many years. The thoughts, concepts and suggestions that I express in this management guide are a direct result of the sum of this experience.

My conversations with my talented niece Vanessa, recently promoted to a management position, prompted me to focus my thoughts on this important subject. Thank you, Vanessa.

And, very special thanks to the women in my life, Vilma, Jody and Mimi for your unconditional support and love.

Table Of Contents

Preface 1

Management — Styles 3

    Theory X 4

    Theory Y 5

    Ego and Empathy 6

The Style Best for You 9

    Manager as Leader 11

The Inspiration Manager 14

The Autocratic Manager 17

Hiring — Firing How to Do It 19

Create A Clear Job Description 23

A Guide to Setting Goals 25

Plan Your Work Work Your Plan 28

Conducting a Performance Review 31

Positive Meetings — 10 Tips 34

Giving Praise and Criticism 37

Projection Is Dangerous 40

Being Friends with Subordinate 43

Recommended Reading 45

About the Author 47

Preface

50 years of active management have taught me that there are a relatively small number of basic things that one must do as a manager that will make the difference between success and the lack thereof. It isn't complicated, in fact, when you read what I have written here you may say; "Hey, that's not very difficult" or perhaps all I'll do is ratify what you're doing right now. In putting my advice on paper, I have tried to keep it succinct, not wordy nor redundant. Many of the points I make may be familiar to you or seem simplistic or even trite. But they are fundamental to your success as a manager, as a leader.

What I have learned over the years comes from in-the-field experience as a manager, both from my successes and failures. I have always tried to learn from my mistakes and build upon my success. My experience informs me that as a manager you're not just managing a business; your true task is managing people: leading, inspiring, mentoring, counseling, coaching, instructing, directing and, perhaps most importantly, motivating the individuals on your team to achieve a common goal.

Successful management is an everyday job. You should be aware that you are under scrutiny by subordinates and perhaps from top management, the board, lenders, investors as well as your organization's clients. All of whom are observing you and making judgments as to your management style, your leadership ability, and, of course, your overall performance.

The ten suggestion that I offer in the following pages are just my version of *Management 101*. Implement them and I believe that they will serve to make you a better, more successful manager.

Management – Styles

If you're looking for the "right" management style to adopt as your model, sorry, there is no "right" management style. However, there are a few basic styles that can be adopted in managing and I'll outline the two most used as well as their derivative forms. But the management style that fits you best, that will make you a more effective manager, depends on what you are most comfortable with. That's the one that will work best for you.

Most of today's styles of management derive from the seminal work done in the 1960's by Douglas McGregor. McGregor was a management professor at the MIT Sloan School of Management and later president of Antioch College. It was at MIT that he developed his landmark *Theory X and Theory Y of Management*. He later wrote an excellent book on management, *The Human Side of Enterprise* which expanded on his Theory X and Theory Y styles of management

Theory X

McGregor's Theory X management style describes an authoritarian style of management, where the manager gives instructions and keeps a close check on each employee and demands compliance. It assumes that employees are not motivated, and that they do not like working.

His theory is based on these assumptions: the typical employee is lazy and dislikes work, is not ambitious and dislikes responsibility and therefore needs to be told what to do and monitored closely. McGregor concludes that the employee is indifferent towards the company's fundamental interest and has no loyalty to the organization.

Therefore, Theory X managers are required to control employees, manage their efforts, motivate them to modify their behavior to comply with the company's objectives. The employees, under Theory X management, must be persuaded, threatened, motivated by rewards, punished for under performance, and closely controlled to get their jobs accomplished. It is an authoritarian, top-down style of management.

Theory Y

McGregor's Theory Y style of management relies on a participative style of management, where the manager assumes that the employees are self-directed and self-motivated to accomplish mutually agreed to objectives. It proposes that they are interested in achieving goals and desire positive recognition for doing so.

This theory says that the average worker does not inherently dislike work, it proposes that employees are creative and self-motivated and like to take on responsibility. It argues that employees are self-directed and therefore the threat of punishment is not a necessary, nor a productive means for achieving the desired results.

McGregor believes that the average person is, in fact, ambitious, willing to take responsibilities, takes pleasure in engaging in creative endeavors and takes satisfaction in accomplishing goals.

Theory Y proposes that employee's commitment to accomplishing objectives is determined by the rewards, psychological as well as income, associated with their achievement.

Ego and Empathy

Dr. Herbert Greenberg, awhile a professor of psychology at Rutgers University published a study in the *Harvard Business Review* wherein, he discussed the role of Ego and Empathy in the context of business activity.

Dr. Greenberg postulated that successful managers and sales representatives conducted their interpersonal relationships with equal amounts of Empathy and Ego.

He defined *Empathy* as the ability to feel as the other person does in order to be able to better understand their position in order to more effectively conduct a business relationship. Having empathy does not mean being sympathetic. One can know what the other fellow feels without agreeing with that feeling. But a manager simply cannot manage productively without the invaluable and irreplaceable ability to get meaningful feedback from the person he or she is dealing without empathy.

The second of the basic qualities Dr. Greenberg found was absolutely needed by a good manager is *Ego*. The drive that makes him/her want and need to achieve in a personal way and not merely for the money to be gained. The term "ego" is too often used as a pejorative descriptor of someone's personality. It is frequently used to describe a person who is self-centered and insensitive to the feelings of others. However, in the context of management, the ego driven person is someone who has an innate drive to be successful, to win, to fulfill his/her personal need. For ego driven managers winning provides a powerful means of enhancing the ego. His/her self-esteem improves dramatically by virtue of winning and diminishes with failure.

Successful Managers work to exercise in managing their team a balance of equal amounts of Ego and Empathy.

The Style Best for You

You may find that you will need to modify your management technique to fit certain circumstances or, more likely, to manage different people with unique personalities on your team who will respond better to a different management style.

I have a *Zoo Theory* of management. It asks that you see your team as a zoo filled with different animals each of whom have different characteristics, appetites and behaviors. The lions like red meat, the elephants eat plants, the monkeys like bananas - you get the point. Like the zookeeper you'll get best results when you recognize the cultural, personality, motivational differences of the members of your team. When managing a diverse group of people, it is vital to deal with them as individuals, recognizing their differences. To deal effectively with the differences of your team members it is most productive to adopt a blended style of management.

No matter the style, one thing needs to be consistent and that's your role as a leader. It is always important to show leadership; in both word and deed. You need to lead by example; what you do and say counts. Leaders determine the character of the organization. Management and Leadership are inseparable: good managers are strong leaders. They perform at a high level of professionalism, act with integrity, have an interest in their employees, show enthusiasm and have passion for what they do.

Below I have summarized several other styles of management that can be implemented in conjunction with either the Theory X or Theory Y management styles. You will tend to be comfortable in one them but keep in mind there will be times that you will need to adopt another style when a set of circumstances calls for modification of your basic style. While being consistent in your management style is important, flexibility is also needed. But be careful in changing management styles, do it rarely and only when it is really needed.

Manager as Leader

While a good part of the job of a manager may be administrative; dealing with things and systems, it is your leadership that motivates the people on your team and inspires them to achieve their individual goals as well as those of the organization. An important part of the manager's job is to foster a workplace environment that encourages cooperative effort, where employees feel part of a team, share common goals and strive for achievement.

However, in today's workplace much needs to be done to create the desired positive, cooperative, productive environment.

In a recent study done by OC Tanner Research found these disturbing results:

❖ 79 percent of employees who quit their jobs claim that a lack of appreciation was a major reason for leaving
❖ 65 percent of workers reported that they weren't even recognized once in the last year
❖ 82 percent of employees feel their supervisor doesn't recognize them for the work they do
❖ 60 percent say they are more motivated by recognition than money

Obviously, for these dissatisfied employees, if their managers had given them the recognition they had earned, had shown genuine appreciation and acknowledge superior performance it would have reduced turnover, created a positive energy that would have significantly produced better results. Clearly positive recognition must be earned. Therefore, it is incumbent on management to clearly define what they expect from their employees; their goals and objectives, and how their performance is directly linked to recognition. In order for recognition to drive results, it must be earned. The individuals on the team must know what is expected of them as members of a team and be in agreement with the goals. When they are aligned with management as to what needs to be accomplished it becomes a catalyst for driving positive results.

Managers must overcome their hesitancy to recognize and reward superior performance. By giving recognition for superior performance you will build an engaged team that works hard to delivers positive results and it will serve to create a workforce that takes pleasure in what they do.

The Inspiration Manager

This style can be very effective for the manager who sees himself/herself as mentor, teacher, a collaborative leader. This manager sets the tone of the organization. He/she imparts to the team the overall goals to be achieved, gets buy in from the individuals on the team, and gives clear direction on how they are to go about achieving those goals. This is not a hands-off system, rather it is a constructively guided method.

The inspirational manager articulates the vision of the company, makes it clear to the employees and provides direction toward achieving that vision. Having expressed the vision and worked with the team in setting goals, both for the organization and the individuals comprising the team the leader then steps back, allowing the employees to do their job.

In this management style the manager monitors progress, offers encouragement, recognition and praise when deserved, is available to help, guide and mentor. An important attribute of this style is that the manager is fair yet firm in dealing with subordinates. This model demands that the manager be aware of employees' progress and is prepared to step in when needed.

This manager strives to be seen as a colleague rather than a "boss". He/she wants to be perceived by the team as a "people person". In this style building relationships with subordinates as important as their performance.

He/she strives to foster cooperative, collaborative working relationships with and among subordinates. The manager acts as coach and when needed will show an employee how things should be done. This management style generates a high level of good feeling in the workplace and high morale among the staff. It can be a positive style to utilize, especially where the work product is creative.

However, there needs to be a clear understanding and agreement of the goals and objectives by the individuals making up the team, so they understand that under this collegial system there are goals and objectives to be accomplished.

A manager who merges inspirational with collegial styles motivates his/her team members by helping them to increase their skills thus providing them with the opportunity for professional growth, which serves to foster productivity, enhance their self-esteem and pride in accomplishment.

This management style encourages individual innovation, builds positive morale, prided in accomplishment and employee self-esteem. with the opportunity for professional growth, which serves to foster productivity, enhance their self-esteem and pride in accomplishment.

The Autocratic Manager

The autocratic manager follows the style as described by McGregor in his Theory X. The manager gives orders and expects them to be followed. This is a top-down style in which the goals of the organization and for those individuals on the team are determined by the manager.

Frequently this type of manager is a micromanager, watching every detail of the process and offering instructions on its execution. It is the rare individual who likes his/her every move watched, criticized or commented on. While the autocratic manager may be quite knowledgeable in the field this style may not be conducive to imparting his/her expertise to team members; in fact, the advice or instruction, however valuable, may be rejected because of the nature of its delivery.

Employee morale under this structure is frequently stressed and individuals on the team have a high level of dissatisfaction. Academics who study the relationship between employee satisfaction and productivity have found that productivity suffers in an organization where stress is high, and employees are unhappy with their work situation. Under this top down management style, the organization frequently suffers a high rate of employee turnover. Turnover is costly to the organization in terms of lost productivity, low morale among remaining staff and actual expense.

However, there are circumstances in which the autocratic management style gets results and is called for. In times of crises a strong hand and decisive decision making may be needed. When needed implement it but be aware that this is a management style that may not serve well the organization over the long term.

Hiring – Firing; How to Do It

Be slow to hire but fast to fire. It is important for you to take your time in recruiting, interviewing, checking references and getting to know a candidate before making an offer. All too often when pressed to fill an open position we skip a couple of these steps. Every time I've rushed the hiring process, I came to regret it. Making a good hiring decision is well worth the effort. The measure of a good manager starts with the ability to hire well. Invite others to join you in the interviewing process, they may pick up a nuance that you missed. Take the hiring process seriously, it is one of the most important decisions you will make as a manager.

Some of the basic questions to ask a prospective employee are: Tell me about yourself? What do you consider your strengths? How about the other side of that question: What are your weaknesses? Why are you interested in this job? What have you heard about the company? How do you handle stress and pressure? What are you passionate about?

The discipline here is for you to be quiet and listen carefully to the candidate's responses. Evaluate their ability to clearly articulate a thoughtful answer. Were they prepared for the interview? Did they know anything about the job, about your company? Take note of the candidate's composure under the pressure of an interview.

We all have a natural inclination to hire people similar in look and cultural background to ourselves. Recognize and resist this tendency. Keep an open mind in your recruiting process; the best candidate may be quite different from you in background, race, sex or ethnic origin. But may, in fact, be the right person for the job. Be disciplined in the process and don't let your personal biases impact your hiring decisions.

We are all human and make mistakes. In the case of having hired someone who turns out to be an underperforming employee terminating him/her sooner rather than later is best for both the employee and the company. Keeping on an underperforming employee sends a negative message to the team about your acceptance of underperformance. Many of us are conflict avoidant and dislike the confrontational aspect of firing an employee but it comes with the job.

Keep in mind taking action to terminate sooner rather than latter will be best for the organization and most probably for the employee as well.

When you have the need to terminate an employee be sure to have a witness present, do not engage in a debate as to the details of why they are being let go. A simple statement that you have decided that it is just not working out and it will be best for the employee and the company to separate. Be sure to retrieve, keys, passes and any office equipment and materials used by the ex-employee. Prior to the termination meeting change his/her computer password and after the meeting the employee should be allowed, in the presence of someone from HR, to gather any personal belongings and then escorted from the premises.

Create A Clear Job Description

An important starting place for a new hire is for them to understand clearly and completely what is expected of them. The best way to be sure of their understanding is to have a very clear, written job description, what the job entails and what is expected of each employee. It should be given together with a company manual making clear the company's policies and procedures. Let the new hire read the job description on their own. Then go over it with each individual employee to be sure of their understanding of what is expected of them and get their agreement as to your expectations.

Clarity here is very important for both you, the manager, and for the new employee. It will prevent future misunderstandings. What you want to avoid is hearing the employee later telling you, or worse, a co-worker: "but that's not my job to do". An unhappy employee is an unproductive employee; and you don't want one of those on your team. Avoid this situation by being very clear from the very start as to what is expected as to work, dress code, the employee's work schedule, reporting lines and the company's HR policies.

From time to time you may need to change the job description. Discuss the proposed modifications in detail, one-on-one, with the employee and then confirm the new job description to paper and go over it with the employee. It is important to be sure that the employee understands and agrees on the modification of their duties. It's a good idea to document the change, give it in writing to the employee and place a copy it the employee's file. If this sounds bureaucratic, it is, but doing this will help to avoid misunderstandings in the future.

A Guide to Setting Goals

It has been my experience that employees like to set goals and even better, they take pride and pleasure in achieving them. The key here is be sure their goals are reasonable and achievable.

My preference is to utilize a bottom up goal setting process wherein you have your employees set their own goals, present them to you and you then review their goals with the employee to be sure that the goals they're proposing are fair, doable and reasonable. This is important because an employee not achieving his/her established goals is a problem for the employee as well as the manager.

A top down process wherein you hand out the goals can work as long as those goals are in a doable range and you get agreement by the employee. You need to avoid a disconnect between the company's idea for goals and those that the employ thinks are reasonable; either too high or too low. Goals that are mutually agreed to lead to enhanced performance. Frequently, some part of the employee's compensation will be tied to goal attainment therefore reaching a mutual agreement on goals becomes even more important. The individual and team goals should be posted at each team members workstation. Doing this will serve as a positive, constant reminder of what needs to be done.

By instituting a system of goals, you are establishing a means of objective accountability in measuring employee performance rather than subjective evaluation. As humans with our inherent emotional tendencies we too often make evaluations and judgments that are not fact based, rather driven by emotion. How often have we have heard: "I go with my gut" or "I have a good feeling about this". Sometimes management decisions made based upon these instinctive drivers work out but having a factual basis for decision-making is the more professional path. Reasonable goals for your individual team members as well as the organization are an important element in having a well performing organization.

If you put into place a goals system, it is imperative that you establish a regular review of progress on achieving those goals. Be sure to share positive progress. If the goals, group or individual, are not being achieved do your best to determine why and work together on problem and seek a solution, then implement it. But, don't threaten the team nor individuals; rather work with them to understand what needs to be done to improve. Threats are, in the long term, counterproductive. Once a get-back-on-track plan is developed implement the changes needed to accomplish the goals. Monitor progress on a regular interval and offer appropriate feedback.

Plan Your Work – Work Your Plan

Success in almost any endeavor depends on a rationally conceived, well thought-out plan. Be it for an individual member of your team, the entire team, or for yourself; having a work plan is a critical element in getting the job done.

The work plan is tactical while goals are strategic. It may take the form of a daily, weekly or longer term "what do I need to accomplish" list on a yellow pad or a digital to do list on a laptop or mobile device. No matter the format what counts is the thought that goes into the development of your work plan and the checking off those items as they are accomplished. Many successful managers draft their week's plan Sunday evening so that come Monday morning they are set to work their plan. In mt opinion your imparting this habit to subordinates can be helpful to them and to the productivity of the organization.

Your subordinates work plans are a powerful tool for channeling their effort, and for the manager to monitor progress and to keep the employee maintaining focus. In the beginning it may beneficial for your team members to share with you their proposed written work plan. And, after some give and take, you need to sign off on their plan. Once a work plan is mutually agreed upon it needs your regular monitoring. To keep aware of the plan's progress you need to have in place a system wherein you hold one-on-one sessions with subordinates at regular intervals to review their progress on their "work plan". The effectiveness of your regular reviewing is enhanced by an open, honest exchange between you and the team member.

The review sessions need to be based upon the offering of well-earned praise for tasks accomplished and positive advice - not negative criticism - for those items still to be done on the work plan list. This offering of advice can be difficult to accomplish as all too often suggestions are perceived as negative. What you want to achieve is positive, helpful guidance clearly focused on helping the employee keep on track with what he/she needs to accomplish.

Conducting a Performance Review

Many employees view their review sessions negatively. They resent them as a negative experience and frequently consider them as a waste of their time. In my opinion this is because all too often the manager conducting the review goes into the review session looking for issues or behaviors to criticize. A performance review does not need to be a negative exercise. It should be structured in a manner that is framed to be productive and helpful for both parties.

Regular reviews, no more than twice a year, conducted one-on-one with individual team members can be a positive exercise if done constructively. How does one change the perception of the review session from negative to positive?

The first step is to open the review with a sincere statement about some positive aspect of the employee's work. If you can't find something positive to say go back and read again Chapter 2. If there is nothing positive to mention; you should question, why is this person still working for you.

Assuming that there are positives in this person's performance, mention them at the start of the review. Be generous with your praise. Research studies confirm that for many persons praise is as good as, or even better, than money. And, most importantly, giving positive recognition sets the tone for the rest of the review as a positive counseling session.

The areas that need improvement can be positioned as your helping the employee to improve, coaching, rather than criticism. It may be productive to ask: "if you were sitting in my chair what would be your evaluation?" The employee may have an insight with regard to an issue that you may not have thought of, and self-evaluation may be more helpful than your observational issues.

The language you use is critical to a positive session so try to keep from using negative words. Be aware of your tone of voice and body language during the review session. Bookend the session by closing the review by repeating the positive comment that you opened the review session with.

Writing up your notes from the review session will prove helpful since in the next session you can track improvement or lack thereof.

Positive Meetings – 10 Tips

A key issue managers need to deal with is group meetings. How often, how long, what should be covered. There is no question that occasional meetings with your entire team are important. Properly planned and informative they can be a positive experience. They should be used to inform, update, motivate and congratulate.

However, recent research clearly indicates that one of the predictors of success for managers was that those who held frequent individual meetings with the people that reported to them were the most effective managers. One-on-one meeting are much more productive; for the employee as well as the manager. All too often the group meetings become a platform for the manager to demonstrate his/her position of power. This display of power, of ego, can be a turn off for meeting participants. When needed keep meetings informative and as brief as possible. My suggestion is to keep group meetings to a minimum.

Here are ten suggestions for conducting a more productive group meeting.

1. Plan the session in advance; know what you want to achieve and what you plan to say.
2. Have an agenda, distribute it in advance to the attendees.
3. Stick with your agenda. Don't let the session get diverted.
4. Have a set time for the meeting; start on time and try to keep the session under an hour.
5. For best results hold the meeting first thing in the morning. Preferably at a location away from the office where there will be less distractions.

6. Require participants to shut off their phone (not just silence the ringer).
7. Keep the session positive. Give an update as to progress. If there is bad news to report do your best to be clear about the reasons why and what your plan is to correct the situation.
8. Be careful about asking for questions; the meeting can quickly get out of your control and instead of the positive session you intended. Don't let it turn into a complaint session. If you're asked a difficult question, try to answer it directly with the person who asked but do so after the meeting.
9. Never single out an individual for criticism in a public setting in front of peers. If criticism is called for do in private behind a closed door; one-on-one.
10. However, singling out someone for praise at the meeting is a very positive thing to do and will serve a positive motivator for the employee as well as the others attending the meeting.

Do your best to follow these ten suggestions and you'll find your group meeting to be much more productive.

Giving Praise and Criticism

Giving deserved, sincere, praise to an employee is a powerful management tool. We all welcome and seek, positive recognition for the work we are doing. For many it is just as important as our financial compensation. The positive impact of praise given in front of peers multiplies its positive impact. However, the praise must be well deserved; based upon a significant contribution to the company's goals and objectives. Positive recognition is a powerful motivator. Don't trivialize it by offering recognition for minor accomplishments. Doing so will only diminish the value of future recognition.

It is very important for the manager to offer praise in front of peers but only criticize in private. When criticism is needed invite the person into a private place or outside the workplace and be clear about the situation. Welcome the employee's feedback and seek a solution to the issue at hand.

You need to be aware of each of your employee's cultural, sex and age differences as you engage in a constructive criticism session. These differences call for sensitivity on your part as you discuss with the employee the problem and together seek solutions. Your goal is to keep the session positive, constructive and to be beneficial for the employee and the company.

Of all the tasks that a manager is required to perform this one is near the top of the list in terms of difficulty. But there will be occasions where it absolutely needs to be done. Don't put it off. Delay in resolving a troublesome situation with an underperforming employee will only make it worse and more difficult to fix. And, you can be sure that other members of the organization are well aware of the problem with the person who needs to be counselled. Not facing the issue and in a timely manner taking this person aside for a candid and direct session says to the rest of the team that you are accepting of his/her behavior. Implicit is the message: "not to worry, you too can get away with it". In summary: both Praise and Criticism are valuable, effective management techniques. But both need to be used with care. You will have the occasion for to use each of them. Don't hesitate to do so.

Projection Is Dangerous

Projection may be one of the more difficult personal behaviors for a manager to change. It is important for the manager to suppress his/her personal feelings, biases, beliefs and not project them on to your employees. Your learned attributes are pretty much set in stone. It is human nature to believe that other people will, or should, think as you do, believe what you believe, behave like you do.

Sadly, this is not the case. Each of us has our own unique set of characteristics, so it is important that you realize that your employees do as well. And theirs will, for sure, be very different from yours. Yours won't change and neither will those of your team members. We are all different, different cultures, preferences, beliefs that have an impact as we deal with our employees. (please refer to my zoo analogy in Chapter 1.)

Our differences need to be recognized and respected. As a manager it is unrealistic and counterproductive for you to see your employees as clones of yourself. Projecting your set of characteristics and beliefs on an employee is rarely accurate. You must make an effort to become aware of their background, cultural makeup and character. Taking these factors into consideration as you deal with your employees in a business context is critical and will prove to be productive.

Of course, you need for your subordinates to fit in to your company's culture. Your challenge is to motivate them to accomplish mutually agreed upon goals. But, recognize that the they will best do so within the framework of their personal cultural makeup. Things like hair style, dress, tattoos, language, personal space, diet are frequently cultural attributes that demand recognition by manager. Only when they negatively impact productivity should they become an issue.

As a manager you should strive to rely on facts to make your decisions while being aware that there is a human factor in how those facts will be perceived by subordinates and as we know too often perception becomes reality.

Being Friends with Subordinate

Effective managers don't make friends with subordinates. Doing so makes effective managing very difficult. Can you have solid, respectful relationships with your employees? Yes. In fact, that is a positive behavior to engage in. Doing so is beneficial and conducive to building a cohesive, well-functioning team.

But, having a real friendship with team members is problematic. As a person you will consciously or unconsciously favor friends over others on the team. This is nothing but trouble. It will build resentment and jealousy, either obvious by others on the team, or worse, negative feelings held under the surface. Even if you make an effort to deal fairly and equally with all members of your team the perception will be that you favor your friends.

This is a difficult issue when you are promoted from within an organization where you had friends to becoming that team's manager. You will need to explain to your friends that circumstances have changed. You are now a manger with a different set of responsibilities and therefore your personal relationship needs to change as well. It may be difficult for them, but you hope that they will understand that you are their boss and that they must respect that fact and understand and accept the new circumstance.

To avoid the problems that friendship will bring you need to draw a clear, bright line as to your interfacing with team members. Socializing is out. No going out for with team members for "Happy Hour". No favoritism. No weekend socializing. No intimate relationships. No going to lunch with old friends on the team

In summary: no friendships with team members. Good managers keep it professional at all times.

Recommended Reading

Here is a list of books that I believe will provide you with additional insight and instruction on both management and leadership. Some of them are classics, dating back to the sixties and others more contemporary.

They each offer their unique perspective on management. Since a core issue in successful management is the art of dealing with people. Therefore, the basic issues will never change.

Theory X and Y by McGregor

In Search of Excellence by Peters

The Effective Executive by Drucker

Eupsychian Management by Maslow

The One Minute Manager by Blanchard & Johnson

14 Points for Management by Drucker

The Coaching Habit by Stamier

First Time Manager by Belker, McCormick & Tapchik

Purple Cow by Godin

About the Author

Herbert M. Levin

Levin is a well-respected, experienced, broadcast executive with many years of successfully managing major market radio stations. Perhaps best known for his pioneering work in Spanish language radio, Mr. Levin was the founder Spanish language radio stations WQBA – *La Cubanisima,* 1140 AM & WQBA - *SuperQ,* 107.5 FM, which under his direction became two of the country's most successful Spanish language radio stations. *SUPER-Q,* was America's first bi-lingual, bi-cultural FM. He was also founder of Miami station *Radio Suave,* WSUA. Expanding into the New York Metro market Levin took over the leadership of WADO and re-branded the station as La *Campeona* which soon became one of the county's legendary Hispanic stations. WADO's format was changed to news/talk. It became a radio station that not only informed but aggressively advocated on behalf of the New York area's large and diverse Hispanic population.

He was the creator of the concept and co-founder of *Radio UNICA,* America's first satellite delivered Spanish language, long-form, news/talk national radio network. *Radio UNICA* was considered by many to be a powerful unifying force within America's large Hispanic community. Levin was executive producer for the documentary: *CUBA; La Generación del Cambio.* And is currently acting a production consultant for an in-development TV series: *EXILE.*

He served for six years as an Adjunct Professor of Marketing at the Florida International University's School of Business & Organizational Sciences, teaching *Case Studies in Marketing Management*. A believer that research is a critical first step for successful business decision making, he has conducted numerous research studies, both quantitative and qualitative for a diverse range of clients: including several universities, media entities, consumer product companies and political candidates.

A graduate of the Pennsylvania State University with a BS degree in Marketing, Mr. Levin is also a graduate of the National Association of Broadcasters Management Development Program given by the Harvard University Graduate School of Business.

Levin is available to speak at your company meeting or association conference.

Contact: hmlconsultant2011@gmail.com

www.ingramcontent.com/pod-product-compliance
Lightning Source LLC
Chambersburg PA
CBHW041109180526
45172CB00001B/182